# Off the Written Track

Payal Das

Presentation by *BookLeaf Publishing*

Web: www.bookleafpub.com

E-mail: info@bookleafpub.com


ISBN: 9789358731064

First edition 2024

# DEDICATION

"He's more myself than I am. Whatever our souls are made of, his and mine are the same." - Emily Brontë, *Wuthering Heights*

For Sap, forever my champion

# ACKNOWLEDGEMENT

I will be forever thankful to
Dadu, for making me dream...
Dida, for believing in me...
Baba-Ma, for letting me fly...
Kutu, for keeping me grounded...

# Stark White Walls

Stark white walls,
That's what I want to be
To your long-stemmed rose in the corner
Single, special, mine,
When it rains, and trust me, it does every day,
You know I am the droplets,
Sliding down the windowpane that is you,
The sighs in our separate rooms, mist up
the glass...
When the wind touches your skin,
I get the shivers, and when I falter,
You make up my mind for me.
When the sun hits my face, and with
closed eyes,
I embrace the warmth,
Your eyelashes are tinged golden by the rays...

A heartbeat here, a prayer there, a white knuckle
here, a closing of fist there,
A half-stolen glance, a furtive touch,
Your face breaks into a smile, and maps the lines
on my hand...
I whisper your name, the air around you
comes alive,
You whisper my name, and lo, there are fireflies,

Time and space and all that jazz,
In our language, we converse,
And as new leaves grow on old potted plants,
We will soon weave more stories…
A hard day's night under a
blanket of memories…

# Drown

The air settles inside the room
As if it's heavy and tired
Sighing, unloads its burden
And the room becomes one shade darker.
There's nothing to be seen here,
You're lucky if you hear a noise
Time glides by the cracked windowpanes.
I glide inside, footsteps no more a thing
There's no steady drip of water
Not that familiar rattle of the table fan,
Light sometimes fights its way in
And finds the dust particles
Suspended from a past
I don't recollect at all.
My veins don't throb anymore
My eyes gaze at the shadows;
They come in wave after wave
But I have learned to cry in silence.
My complaints play shapes on the walls
Solitude is a mercy, is it?
The only chance to stay afloat
My voice muffled by my fist
Here, at last, I drown…

# Look at the Sky

Look at the sky with me

Before the wind comes
Before the clouds dissolve
Before the rain hits
And my windowpane is a blur.

Before the day is gone
Before the birds take flight
Before the puddles dry
And night drops its cover.

Before the grey turns to ink
Before we let go of things
Before we spread our wings
And merge into each other
Brush strokes in watercolour.

Look at the sky and surrender.

# Loneliness

What do you know of
loneliness?
Spotting an unfortunate bird
Sharing the burden
Of a half-escaped sigh
And lowered eyes,
Trying not to let
The couple's entwined fingers
Blur your vision.

What do you know of
loneliness?
Dropping the bags
The load of another day
Gone by, unfulfilled
Eating food that's half as bad
As the stale air inside the room
That has known only one person.

What do you know of
loneliness?
Faces all around,
In cubicles, in train compartments,
In this cubby hole
And yet faces disappear
An appeal in my eyes,

The hands raised hesitantly
Eyes glued to
Reruns of drama seasons.

And there's only you and I
Lightyears away
For what reason
For what reason
For what reason…

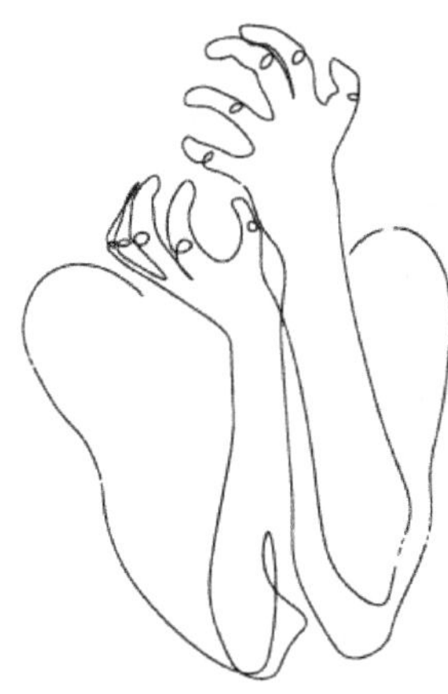

# A Dream for Ages

The lines on my hands are mostly faded
The symmetry is gone,
Hidden under wrinkles and calluses
But they remember how your hands used to
mould into mine
They remember the warmth, every bit of it
And the terrible cold, of loss...

My eyes are in a web now
I don't see so well, unwilling prisoner
of crow's feet
I no longer read the letters you wrote to me
But at the end of another tiring day,
At the end of the meaningless games
At the end of all entertainment, parched
My eyes find you, and remember
You, in every detail, as if nothing ever changed
As if you are still holding the light for me
At the end of this tunnel
My eyes, as they hold you still,
And cry for you, when images do not
become real...

I feel the hollowness inside,
As memories rush past, and it gets more and
more difficult
To differentiate
As time melts into puddles, and people's faces
blend into each other
I desperately clutch your photos
I hold on to all our milestones
Your face is still as clear as daylight
As serene as a mountain stream
I can hear your laughter from miles away
Piercing my heart
Singing a melancholy note, like the wind
blowing through the pine trees
I would have liked to walk some more with you
Up and down the winding mountain roads
Through the ups and downs of life
I wanted to grow old with you
It's a dream I still dream...

# Your Voice

It's just the way your voice feels
No, not like they describe it in novels
Not like dripping honey,
Or rumbling thunder
Or even the rain that comes at the end of it.
Your voice feels like the finality
When it rains so hard that the world folds itself
around you,
The tumult outside leads to a quietness
That resonates like waves receding from
the shore,
If darkness at the end of a tiring day
had a sound.
When I close my eyes hoping to open them in a
parallel world
Where you are,
Forever with me.
Your voice is like my patchwork quilt,
The one which instantly brings back memories
Of cozy nights, coffee beans, and comfort.

When the momentary ice in your voice melts
And I can feel my way in again,
I hold your hand and run across
The familiar cobblestone paths in our
conversations.

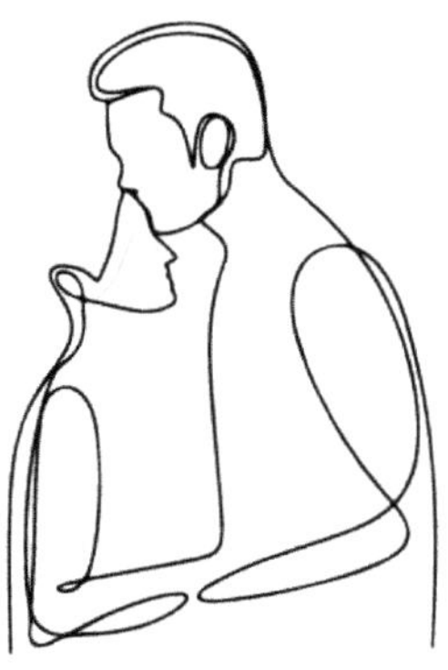

# The Forest

I see it often now
The forest
You know, of things lost
Or discarded.
I see the path clearly
Trees, bent with neglect, showing the way
Leaves, dry and rustling, sigh beneath
my feet...
Then it flickers and disappears
As I step back
Into yet another illusion
Of a happy life
Of fulfillment.
The forest remains, though
Like a shadow, ever-spreading
With every heartbreak
And ghosts of past memories
The skeletal beasts of the forest whisper;
With every tear
And scar tissue
The ravens carry my unsaid words
Through the forest of un-belonging.

My reality, sad if you may, is drifting away
Bonds are mirror images of how they were
before
There's nothing here to hold onto...

The forest looms large and breathes heavy
And waits for its next resident.

# That Part of You

Your walls hold all my secrets
Your sheets my sighs
Your windows open to my soul
And close, at the end of my lies.

Lies that I tell every day
Lies that keep up my mask
Lies that show I am fine
Lies that slip away in the dark.

Dark, as my days are without you
Dark, as the walls of my heart
Dark, the depths I want to sink in
And lose myself when your lips part.

Part of me, part of you
Raindrops on the glass
Part of you, part of me
Miracles will come to pass…

# Lockdown Reveries

It's been a month
That I have been home
Not as a momentary visitor
Not on those sanctioned leaves
No planning, no preparations
And it already feels like I had never left.
It was to be a surprise
And yet, the relief in their eyes mirrored mine
A few tears, dropped here and there
As wrinkled brows cleared up,
And anxious hearts reunited.

It's a battlefield outside
And you are in the trenches daily
You don't come home
Isolation is your only company
I saw you twice, thirty days meant nothing
I wait for you, like a letter yet to be written,
And the sun, yet to go down
And the clouds, holding their rage within,
I wait for you, at the end of this deluge.

As the world waits for respite
I wait for you with a silent prayer.

# I Wanted to be a Star

I wanted to be a star
Not the complaint in your voice
Not the disappointment in your eyes
Not the soft dismissal
In the breath of a soundwave
Rudely cut short.

I wanted to be a star
Not the black sheep in the corner
Not the 'let's not discuss' at dinner tables
Not the epitome of arrogance
In the spark of a decision
Operated on, laid bare.

I wanted to be a star
Blazing across the deep dark discontent.

# The Blues

On a half-forgotten afternoon
In a blue corner
You will glance upon a memory
Through a looking-glass
Tinged aqua.
You will see so azure the sky was
How blue the veins under our feet
How blue the dreams in our eyes
How blue the blood that went cold
As the hands were forced to let go
As the blues of rusty weekdays took over
The hour of late goodbyes
Was upon us, once again.
Like being submerged in water
For a moment, reality slips away
I take a deep breath and dive into the blue...
You.

# Lovers' Tiff

My anger, slices across like a lightning bolt
Your fury, blazing like the merciless sun
My silence, calm after the storm of tears
Your silence, deeper than the dark sky
My hurt, stifled and growing
Your indifference, ebbing and flowing
My words, unspoken
Your words, not formed
My pain, runs helter-skelter through my veins
Your pain, runs parallel to mine...

Your hopes, block by block, became a
winding road
My dreams, tuft by tuft, sprouted alongside
Why then
Can't we
Find our way back again?

# Lost in Time

If time stopped then and there,
Would you agree to
Not look at your watch
Or the sun setting or rising
Or how the wind changed its direction
And how the bird flew away with it?
How the grass blended into each other
And how the dogs decided to leave us alone?
How the people went on their way
Their glance not on us anymore?

If time stopped then and there,
Would you know that we were blessed?
For you would be forever here
In this cocoon, bright and joyous
We would be forever young,
Let the world complete millions of revolutions
You and I
Safe in our own rebellion...

If time stopped then and there,
Would you look at me
And hold that smile?
And I could have lived
A thousand namedays

In your shade, in your grace,
In your eyes, the man you see...

For us,
Time listened, blushed, stilled its heart and held
its breath.

# I am She

I begin at the start, I cease at the end
I wait at every crossroad and every bend
The stuff of your sultry dreams
and worst nightmares,
Come be the slave of my stony stares.

I'm the one everyone warned you about
But norms are meant for you to flout
Try all your tactics, attack and defend,
It's no use, I always win in the end.

Wrapped in carpets, I'm the ancient charmer
The bee in your bonnet, the chink in
your armour
Oh how I love, how I lie, on and on...
My black heart pours forth the deadliest poison.

I kill for pleasure, a veritable Bathory!
The angel, the devil, or closer home, Matahari?
I'm the eclipse that shadows you forever
I'm your past, present and future.

I'm like a habit that grows on you
The pestilence, the silence,
That gnaws at and devours you
Oh you can't be saved by any chance.
Regurgitating bits and pieces
Of your red, pulsating heart,
And sweet nothings whispered lightyears ago,
Slashed and pierced by my sinister dart.

I'm the truth from the womb,
I'm the destiny leading to your tomb,
I'm that curse you cannot mend,
I'm your beginning, I'm your end…

# Every Bit of You

The sun dips its fingers
And plays noughts and crosses
On your body
In blood red,
And I peep from my barred windows
For a sliver of that sun
To see the quiver of your lips,
One nanosecond before
You break into a smile
And the sun bursts into a thousand pieces.
Your skin, burnt sienna
My dreams, tinged azure
My thoughts are tendrils
Tangled in the web of your hair
And as I reach out to you
My blues turn lush green
The meadow stretches far between
My soul lies within
The curves I can trace with my eyes closed.
Sunkissed, you and I
My world turned upside down
Doors that lead to nowhere
Yet I sink to the floor, and sink beyond
The green grass, and the softness
Of the canvas that is every bit of you.

# Childhood

It amuses me when you speak of 'childhood',
How lightly you use the word
Things that take you back to your childhood
A collection of long-lost books, or a whiff of a
long-forgotten scent.
But do you know how similar you are to
my childhood?
Magical, joyous, transient...
Those days were once coloured with
my laughter
My dreams shaped them, my tears marked them
There was this ease, of a safe place,
A hideaway, if you may
Where I could disappear, and the world couldn't
touch me.
Everything was special, from raindrops to
patterns on cats' furs, to the shapes of clouds to
new editions of *Chandamama*!
Every day, there was a certain joy in living,
breathing, being,
Wide-eyed wonder was more than enough,
Where the scales tipped for happy memories...

That was childhood, just like you, in my life
Something that I can no longer return to.

# Playing Houses

I wandered lonely,
No, not as a cloud
They are supposed to be fluffy and without a
care
My loneliness, now, that's something
Like a black hole,
Sometimes flickering inside me,
Sometimes threatening to devour me,
And in you walked
And filled up that void
Which had stayed beside me
All my life.

Then mirrors weren't black anymore,
And rainy days took on a meaning of their own,
Sudden smiles did not need a reason
Making up excuses became so easy
Going behind everyone, going with you
Seeing the world, from the doorstep
Of the house you built for me
Where I could play hide and seek with you
Always finding you at the end
Of all my trials and tribulations
A house, not of brick and mortar
But as strong as iron, still.

They are counting our years of playing houses,
But they don't know that our games began eons
ago
Our souls, centuries old,
Running past faces, stuck in our own mazes,
Searching, mistaking, burning, shrieking,
Picking up pieces, and then,
During one final game, with our wisps of breath
Faith hanging by a thread,
We found each other,
A battered piece fit into the other,
And life began, in earnest.

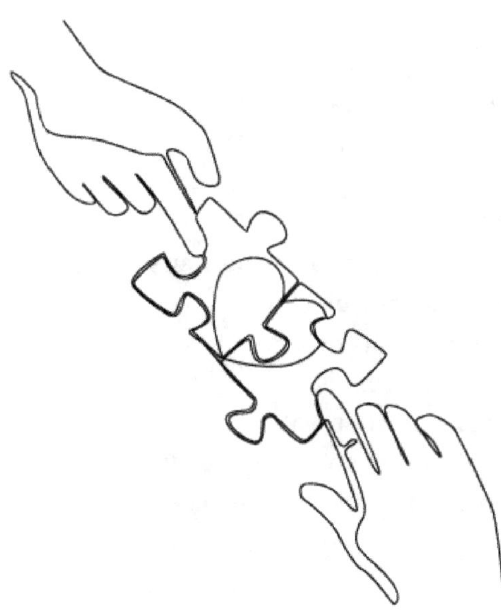

# Dark

Fingers
Skeletal, grubby handprints,
Fingernails, broken...
Rotten, dirty, graffitied, dark...
Scratching, scratching,
At your flawless pink walls,
Scratching at your surface,
Clawing up your sickly sweet bubblegum,
Ensnared.

And the day goes on,
Like any other day,
Silence, all around,
Loneliness, too profound...
Just the creaking,
Disjointed feet on missing stairs,
Just the squeaking,
Rusty fan on its orbit,
Just the screeching,
My nails on your walls,
Dumb, monotonous, bubblegum
My nails and your hollow face, dark...

The walls close in,
Yet the distance grows
The afternoon sun,
Lazy, amorous, meaningless.
And then... dark, that's how it goes...
Buzzing in my ears,
Salty eyes,
Dreamless stare,
Do they suffice?
Drumming inside my head,
Heartache in a lonely bed,
And screaming, scheming, seeming,
Reality invades, menacing... so dark...

A tiny heart,
And its minuscule problems,
Yet this throbbing
Larger than life
I want to dive into endless waters
Never to resurface...
Yet my nails, those grossly curious nails,
Scratch at your surface again,
Your myriad-hued rainbow,
Your pink pretty perfect life,
For one gulp of air,
For some love and care,
Scratch, rip, claw, tear,
Vaudeville and mindless fanfare!

Dark,
All around me, chasing, chasing,
Dark,
Engulfing, overpowering, omnipotent, severe,
Dark,
It's so dark in here…

# Home and Heart

They say that the world is a small place
And yet many a times the sun rose and set
I was yet to find my way home to you
I was yet to know that home could be
Without form, without structure, without roof
and walls
But with a thousand windows and
a billion lights,
Without a fixed address, yet where my roots
have taken hold
Without commodities, beyond conventions,
replete with conversations, at all times of the day
Or a companionable silence, if you may...
I walked miles in search of this home
This home to call my own
To wrap my arms around it and keep it safe
My safe place, in so many words.
And then one rainy day, the world did grow
smaller,
The steps towards you became hurried,
The distance between your heart and mine,
minuscule
I was home...

A dream then, taking shape now
With landmarks and corners and the pitter-patter
of furry paws
It manifests in brick and mortar, yet we float on
a cloud
I part the curtains, sunshine peers in, and
Silhouettes a heart-shaped trio.

And since forever, we have lived and loved.

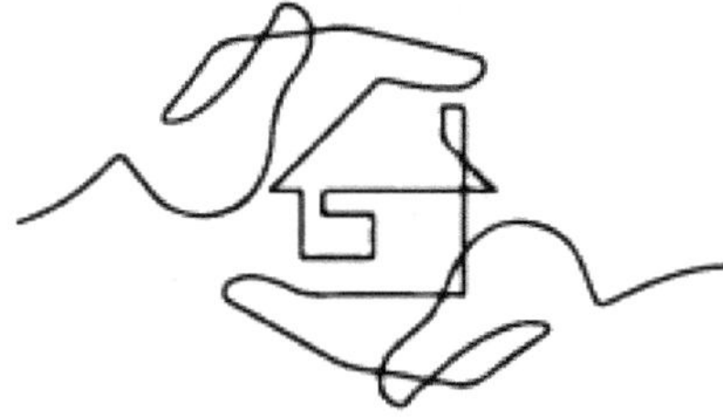

# Milestones

A blank page lies before me
While I try my best to summon the words
That would make the edges curl,
And become indelible
A letter for every memory we make
A word, perhaps, for every emotion we share
The page lies empty, your face becomes clear
On the rain-streaked windowpanes
Of my heart.
And so has it been,
Counting pebbles to milestones
Between despair and relief
And mostly holding on than letting go.
At the start of the journey, fresh-faced and
mischievous
I found your hand and found myself
Across treacherous muddy roads
And many years down the line,
I still find myself every day, feet firmly planted,
My fingertips barely reaching the length
of yours,
The warmth intact, the shade comforting,
In a little place between your world and mine,
Beyond the welcomes and goodbyes.

Here it is, that we meet
We sing a favourite song
And when the song ends,
And day breaks,
And dreams leave our eyes
Here it is, where we build our castles
And our hourglass stories don't lie…

# My Shelter

Shelter
In your eyes
From the harshest of words
And the shadow of failures,
From the all-consuming dark
That is hand-in-hand with loneliness,
From the weight of the world
From the weight of risks taken
From every act of rebellion
And the often tiring consequences.

Shelter
In your arms
In my favourite dishes,
In my room, kept just like before
In my every little thing, perfect and unchanged
The creases on my clothes straightened
Just as you touch my bent-up life
One moment, I am out of sorts
And the very next, it's all in order
And I am back to the rosy days of childhood
The ease and comfort that only you bring.

Shelter
In the concern in your eyes
The questions after my well-being
The worry and the love,
Mixed in equal measure
Just as the dessert you always make
Which you know I crave
And even if your hands are heavy
With the burden of seeing us all through
Safe and sound
You still don't forget to sprinkle
Your blessings and a pinch of your pride
Always rooting for me.
Shelter to me, is you
And after a long day,
Ma, I'm home…

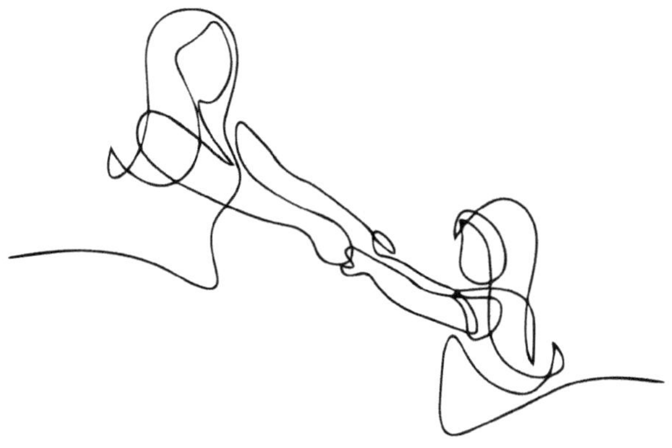